The Canadian Rockies

The pristine wilderness to enjoy, respect & preserve

Text and photographs by

GEORGE BRYBYCIN

GB PUBLISHING

The incredibly warm colours of Mountain Ash, by the Valley of the Ten Peaks. Banff National Park.

The Beautiful Rockies

Many consider the Canadian Rockies to be the most beautiful of Canada's mountains. The chain originates in New Mexico and continues north along the Great Divide. From the U.S. border, the Rockies continue for 1500 km, up to the Liard River near the Yukon border. The chain's average width is from 80 to 100 km. The Foothills flank the Rockies on the east, separating them from the sprawl of the Prairies. To the west, several ranges flank the Rockies, including the Purcell, Monashee and Caribou - all part of the Columbia Mountains. Farther north, past Pine Pass, the Omineca and Cassiar Mountains parallel the Rockies to their north end at the Liard River.

The apex of the Rockies is the majestic Mt. Robson at 3954m in height; the second is Mt. Columbia at 3747m; third is the North Twin at 3683m.

Compared to Canada's highest mountain, Mt. Logan (6050m) in the Yukon, the Rockies are not so high, but they are high enough in their own right: large and wild, they encompass all - as great mountains should.

All the great western rivers originate in the Rockies: the Bow River, the North and South Saskatchewan Rivers flow east to the Atlantic Ocean; the Athabasca, Peace and Liard Rivers all empty into the Arctic Ocean; and, west of the Divide, the Kootenay, Columbia and Fraser Rivers all empty into the Pacific Ocean.

These and other large rivers get their waters from scores of small creeks, which drain the snow and ice-clad mountains. Rainwater is a major factor in water management as well, since it is kept in the forest floor and gradually released into drainages. This is why clear-cut logging is so dangerous for a mountain environment - a non-existent forest cannot hold heavy downpours, so the water rushes down the steep, bare slopes, carrying away soil and causing landslides and floods.

The climate of the Rockies varies from north to south. Along the Great Divide, precipitation is substantial throughout the year - the western slopes get more rain than the eastern. Through several low mountain passes, strong, warm winds blow - melting snow in the winter and making grazing easier for wildlife. Summer temperatures are temperate and pleasant. Winters in the south are cold, in the north, very cold -40° C is not uncommon.

Most of the wildlife in the hemisphere can be found here. The forest, plants and flowers are most impressive in the Rockies' National Parks. Regretfully, outside the Parks, large areas have been logged out and nature devastated.

The Human presence and exploration of the Rockies, is fairly recent. In 1883, the railroad that was pushing west reached Banff, which really opened up the area. Immediately, the area began drawing hardy explorers who needed to know "what was beyond that next mountain." In 1884, the first mountains were ascended. The fad continued, so the Canadian Pacific Railway brought Swiss guides for its hotel guests. Mountaineering took off, and today it is a very popular, enjoyable and healthy sport.

This splendid view of the Athabasca River Valley and Colin Range photographed in early morning, from the summit of Pyramid Mountain (2766m), just north of Jasper. A fine example of the reward one gets for climbing a mountain.
Notice how green the Athabasca River is - its waters comes mostly from glaciers.

Maligne Lake is a well - known sight in Jasper National Park. A large, deep lake of glacial origins, it measures 22km in length,
with an average width of 1.5km. It is flanked, on both sides, by high mountains. The highest, at the far end,
is the Mt. Brazeau Group, where glaciers and an icefield supply the lake with
silty water - hence its green colour.

Above: The wintry Peyto Lake is one of the more pristine lakes of the Central Rockies. Fortunately, no direct trail leads to the lake. Public access for viewing the lake is a platform a good distance away. On the left is Caldron Peak (2917m) with the Mistaya River Valley in the distance. The lake is named for Bill Peyto - early explorer, guide and all - round colourful character.

Left: The marvel of the Rockies - Lake Louise is nestled amongst high, glaciated mountains. On the left is the top of Mt. Lefroy (3423m), and in the center stands the monumental Mt. Victoria (3464m). The lake was discovered by guide/explorer Tom Wilson in 1882, and was named after Princess Louise - fourth daughter of Queen Victoria - in 1884.

The small, but very picturesque Waterton Lakes National Park is located in Southern Alberta, by the U.S. border. This is the only place where the Prairies and the Rockies are not separated by foothills. Since the park is off the beaten track, the human presence is not as overwhelming as in other parks. However, there is a need to enlarge the park to accommodate the areas large wildlife population.

Although they do not roam free - confined to the boundaries of a Paddock - these Buffaloes, or Bison (Bison bison) near Waterton, appear to be doing well. Once there were millions of the great beasts roaming the west. Now there are only a few small herds remaining - in Wood Buffalo National Park and a few other reserves. Bison ranching for profit is becoming fashionable, but at least these magnificent beasts will continue to exist.

The beautiful Bow Lake is situated southeast of the Bow Summit, along the Icefields Parkway. The Wapta Icefield and Bow Glacier to the south,
provide meltwaters and give birth to the Bow River - which flows through the lake, along the Great Divide to Lake Louise, Banff,
and then east, over the Prairies to the Atlantic Ocean. Crowfoot Mountain (3050m) sees its eastern face
in this mirror - like lake in the early morning.

The small, but picturesque Herbert Lake can be found along the Icefields Parkway, just northwest of Lake Louise. The lake is near the Great Divide, which makes for interesting photography because of the very capricious, moody weather. Recognizable mountains in the photo are, from left: Mts. Temple, Fairview, Haddo and Aberdeen.

The bighorn sheep (Ovis canadensis) is a common dweller throughout the Rockies. They live on, or by, steep, craggy rocks - safe from predators. They may fall prey to cougars or wolves when grazing in meadows, or drinking water. This small band is looking attentively up the slope, where a Black Bear has shown up and could pose a threat.

It is hard to imagine anything prettier than a healthy, mixed forest in golden autumn. This is a stand of many - hued poplars, mixed with green coniferous in a forest along the Robson River in Mount Robson Park. High mountains are rainmakers - which is why the area is so lush and rich in forests, plants, flowers and fauna.

On the summit of Fairview Mountain (2744m), a hiker admires the great panorama at first light. From the left are Mts. Haddo, Aberdeen, Lefroy and long, glacier - clad Mt. Victoria (3464m). Victoria Glacier, half - covered in gravel debris, is in the shadow. Fairview Mountain is a small mountain, but provides great views. Banff National Park.

The summit of Fossil Mountain (2946m), situated just east of Deception Pass on the way to Skoki, provides magnificent vistas. The two bulky mountains to the east are Mt. Douglas (3235m.) on the left and Mt. St. Bride (3312m). Both are quite remote and difficult to climb. On the easy, moderate slopes of Fossil Mountain, an avalanche has killed two skiers. Banff National Park.

Above: World - renowned, the turquoise Moraine Lake and the Tower of Babel (2360m) look as great as ever. Geologists speculate that a large rockslide fell from Mt. Babel and dammed the creek, creating the lake. Others say that the pile of rock fell on a glacier in the upper valley and traveled piggyback, down on the glacier until the ice melted away.

Left: High up in a picturesque narrow valley, west of Lake Louise, Lake Agnes nestles peacefully, surrounded by jagged peaks and alpine vegetation. The Devil's Thumb (2458m) dominates the horizon and is an eastern ridge of Mt. Whyte. Mts. Whyte and Niblock can also be climbed from here. Banff National Park.

Along the Icefields Parkway, northwest of the Bow Summit, the Upper and Lower Waterfowl Lakes nestle in the Mistaya Valley. The snowy mountains and half - frozen lake indicate… May. Yes, winter is very long in the Rockies (Peyto Lake is still frozen in June!)
On the left is Epaulette Mountain (3095m) and in the centre are the two Kaufmann Peaks. Banff National Park.

A serene view of the First Vermilion Lake and Mt. Rundle (2998m), in Banff. The three Vermilion Lakes are a rich and diverse ecosystem. Its marshy terrain shelters the rich wildlife. Although the Moose has been eliminated by the human presence, other species thrive here. Waterfowl are well represented.

Walking along a mountain creek, or stream, one can see dozens of waterfalls of varying sizes, cascading waters, small pools and so forth. Lush vegetation is always present along these life - giving waters. Photographing the lively waters is always enjoyable, and a learning experience.

In spite of the northern latitudes, high altitude and harsh mountain climate, there is a rich and plentiful flora here. Summer days are long, with plenty of sunlight. Some plants turn their reproductive cycle in less than two months. The showy Fireweed (Epilobium angustifolium) is common throughout the Rockies. It is found in open, sunny areas.

A glacier carved this little valley just southeast of Moraine Lake, Consolation Valley houses the two Consolation Lakes. This beautiful, hidden valley is flanked by Panorama Ridge to the east, Mt. Quadra to the south and Mt. Babel to the west. Golden Larches are beautiful in the autumn, but the Grizzly Bears, who frequent the area, are unpredictable. Caution is advised.

The most celebrated lake of the Rockies is Lake Louise. It has all the ingredients: emerald glacial waters, lush vegetation and challenging glacier - clad mountains. For the most part, however, the Chateau is behind its fame — a world - class hotel with all the services and amenities necessary for a great holiday.

Mt. Assiniboine (3618m), is the sixth highest mountain in the Rockies. It closely resembles Switzerland's Matterhorn (4506m). Both are world renowned for their height and difficulty in climbing. J. Outram, G. Bohren and C. Hasler were the first to climb the mountain, in 1901. Mt. Magog is on the left.

The Takakkaw Falls (Native Canadian for "splendid") is Yoho National Park's major attraction. It drops over 300m from the high plateau at the west end of the Waputik Icefield and Daly Glacier, into Yoho Valley. The best time to view the falls is in June and July when the snow and ice are melting fast. In the late autumn, the falls is a mere fraction of its summer self.

A classic view of the highest mountain in the Canadian Rockies - monumental, snow - clad Mt. Robson (3954m). The mountain's height creates its own climate. Moisture traveling east from the Pacific Ocean crashes into the mountain, causing generous amounts of rain and snow. This is why the relatively dry Rockies has a rainforest by the Robson. In turn, lush vegetation attracts a diversity of wildlife. This is a real, beautiful wilderness.

East of Mt. Robson and Berg Lake, along the Robson Glacier, a scenic trail leads to Snowbird Pass. Twenty five years ago the glacier reached
down beyond the sloughs shown in the center, and was wide, thick and healthy. It now melts at the rate of 15m per year
and has shrunk in width and thickness, and is covered by dirt particles. Not a very pretty sight, to be sure.
Dominating Robson Pass to the north, is Mumm Peak (2968m) on the right.

Waterton Lakes National Park is known for its exquisite beauty and for its winds. The winds, however, are not all that bad, especially in winter!
Called the Chinook, the western wind brings warm pacific air and melts snow in no time - providing easy access to forage for animals.
Grazing wild animals, from the entire region, migrate here for the winter seeking security in the herd and easy forage.

The first snow of autumn by Mt. Crandell (2377m), in Waterton Lakes National Park, viewed from the north. This small, cozy park is blessed with more scenic delights than many larger parks. Because of the rich wildlife here, it would be beneficial to double the size of the park. Tourists and nature lovers would certainly appreciate that, as would the animals.

The three Vermilion Lakes, just west of Banff, are home to a rich and diverse wildlife. Elk, Deer and Bear still frequent the area.
Sadly, the permanent human presence has driven the Moose away. Smaller animals, rodents and waterfowl still abound.
The Bald Eagle and Osprey can be seen fishing here as well.

The beautiful Valley of the Ten Peaks, dressed in its autumn best as an enthusiastic hiker greets the lofty peaks in early morning. As the area is visited by thousands of people every day, pressure on the wildlife grows. The majestic Grizzly Bear makes its home here - so confrontations between human and beast are possible. Caution is advised.

Above: Twenty five years ago, perhaps five climbers had scaled Mt. Athabasca (3490m) in winter. Things have changed quite a bit. Here, it is "rush hour" on the mountain - eight climbers push on in a splendid winter morning. The summit offers great views of the Columbia Icefield, with Mt. Columbia and both Twins.

Left: Mt. Burgess (2599m) and the emerald Emerald Lake are both synonymous with the splendid Yoho National Park. Small, but filled with major natural features, Yoho is enjoyed year - round. This is a very natural photo - the author avoid using filters or technical tricks.

Above: The several kilometer long, multi - peaked Yellowhead Mountain (2412m), is located just north of Yellowhead Lake, 33km west of Jasper.
Mount Robson Provincial Park. North of the mountain, in the Miette Valley, many lakes dot the unspoiled wilderness.
Reflected here, in Witney Lake, bronzed by the sun.

Left: The picturesque Yellowhead Lake is situated along the Yellowhead Highway, west of Jasper. It abounds in fish, waterfowl and other
aquatic life and is home to the great moose. Mt. Fitzwilliam's (2907m) northwest face is reflected in the still waters of
late afternoon. This quite remote mountain was first climbed in 1917.

The morning mist along Pyramid Lake adorns Pyramid Mountain (2766m) on a splendid autumn sunrise. The large tower on the summit is
a microwave communications facility. The mountain is an easy scramble and was first ascended by renowned explorer
G.B. Kinney, guided by the legendary Conrad Kain, in 1911.

The access road to Moraine Lake is closed during the winter due the threat of avalanches. Access by ski is very pleasant, and the only way to see this paradise in its winter whites. An early start - two hours before sunrise - rewarded the photographer with this picture of winter's end thaw on the lake.

The Forbes Group sprawls for a 100 sq. km southwest from the North Saskatchewan and Howse Rivers' fork. It is dominated by Mt. Forbes (3612m), the seventh - highest elevation of the Rockies, on the right. Lesser Mt. Outram (3252m) is on the left.
This heavily glaciated region is a major climbing area.

The large, glacial Bow Lake is nestled amongst high mountains along the Icefields Parkway, southeast of the Bow Summit. It is just south of here, at the Bow Glacier, where the Bow River is born. The lake is laden with glacial silt and, at certain times of the year, is turquoise green. Snowy Crowfoot Mountain (3050m) forms the background.

This gorgeous palette of nature's colours, west of Grande Cache, along the Smoky River, appears so tranquil and eternal. Further away, one will see a different picture - huge clear cut, devastated areas. The lumber truck on the right is only one of dozens hauling dead trees away every day, year round. Industry desperately needs more cardboard to produce boxes to be half - filled with various products.

This is the summit view from Mt. Burgess (2599m) at first light. The jewel of Yoho National Park, Emerald Lake literally nestles amongst
high mountains. From the left are: conical Mt. Carnarvon (3040m), The President (3138m) and the Vice - President (3066m).
The shadow of Mt. Burgess is on the left. This paradise encompasses diverse
wildlife - moose, bears and loons are not rarities here.

Maligne Lake, located 40km southeast of Jasper townsite, is the major sight, and tourist attraction of Jasper National Park. Surrounded
by high mountains, the lake is 22km long and 1.5km in average width. Hardy explorers canoe to the lake's end,
camp at Coronet Creek and explore this great, wild area.

Nocturnal wonders fascinate painters and photographers alike. While a painter can sketch the scene and paint in his studio, the photographer must deal with the full moon, clear sky, calm water and Grizzly Bears - all at the same time. Here is a multiple - exposure photo of Herbert Lake, northwest of Lake Louise.

Before the fire, this forest was dense and dark, and the forest floor had little vegetation. After the fire, the soil, enriched by the ashes, was quickly colonized by new plant life - mostly Fireweed (Epilobium angustifolium), which strives on disturbed soil like that found after forest fires. It won't be long before the forest comes back, new and healthy - and the plants on the forest floor will gradually vanish. It's nature's way.

The annual festival of colour staged in the Larch Valley, usually in October. The Larch Tree is the only coniferous tree that loses its needles annually. This photo features the valley, just west of Moraine Lake. In the dramatic background are some of the "Ten Peaks" - the glacier - clad one on the left is Mt. Fay (3234m).

The grand panorama viewed from the summit of Mt. Athabasca (3490m). On the left stands Mt. Andromeda; in the center, on the horizon, is the second - highest elevation in the Rockies – Mt. Columbia (3747m); and on the right, are the south slopes of the Snow Dome. Notice two climbers approaching the summit ridge on the right. First ascended by prominent early explorers J.N. Collie and H. Woolley in 1898.

Descending the north icefield of Mt. Athabasca (3490m) after a successful summit climb. Treading between large crevasses and hanging blocks of ice, this simple climb could turn into a very scary business at any time. This photo clearly illustrates what happens when a glacier rolls over a steep rocky hump – it cracks, breaks, crumbles, separates and falls. Glaciers are very dangerous places to visit.

The summit of Sunwapta Peak (3315m) looking west. On the left horizon, looms the huge, white pyramid - Mt. Clemenceau (3658m), the fourth - highest mountain in the Rockies. Sunwapta Peak is a huge mountain just northwest of the Columbia Icefield. It is easily accessible but a toilsome climb. Jasper National Park.

A large cataract on the Kicking Horse River at the west end of Yoho National Park - the Wapta Falls plunges into a misty gorge.
A short hike on a good trail through the moist, dense woods is required to view the falls. Mosquito spray is mandatory
- bear spray is optional. The best time to visit is in early summer, when the water level is high.

A climber approaches the summit of Mt. McArthur (3015m), located northwest of the Little Yoho Valley in Yoho National Park, and first ascended by W.S. Drewry in 1891. A short climb and glacier walk is required to get here. From the left are: The Vice - President, The President, Mt. Kerr and Mt. Carnarvon.

The first snow in the Valley of the Ten Peaks, in early October. When the road is closed for the winter, the only way to see the valley in its white clothes is on skis. A leisurely trip - 2.5 hours up and 1.5 hours back - is very pleasant and rewarding.

Above: Many lakes can be found in Kananaskis Country - some natural, some man - made. This is Upper Kananaskis Lake, a good fishing and boating lake. To the south, mighty mountains flank the lake. They are, from the left: Mt. Foch, Mt. Sarrail and Mt. Lyautey.

Left: Mt. Kidd's (2958m) craggy east face reflected in a small tarn. The mountain is on the right; the lesser peak (2895m) is on the left, 1.5km southwest of the main peak. Many attractive climbing routes lead to the top, mostly from Ribbon Creek Valley. Kananaskis Country.

Great, lush alpine meadows stretch for miles on the east slopes of the Vermilion Range in Kootenay National Park.
The most picturesque area is from Floe Lake, north to the Tumbling Glacier. Many people make
camping trips to admire this very scenic section of the Rockies.

The majestic Bighorn Sheep (Ovis canadensis) are quite common in the Rockies. They are often seen, begging for handouts, along the road. Please do not attempt to feed the wildlife. Not only is it illegal, it also contributes to the deaths of many animals on the roads.

Green Is Beautiful

People, who come from crowded, densely populated areas of the world, are truly impressed when visiting the Rockies. They drive for hours without seeing anything manmade in this beautiful, pristine wilderness. They often fail to realize that all this land is protected by National Park status.

Many of the world's national parks are 50 sq. km in size - Jasper Park, alone, measures 10,878 sq. km. Here's a great and wise idea: let's keep that size or even increase some of the smaller parks like Waterton and Yoho.

Quite often, when one leaves the National Parks, one enters an entirely different world: areas in the Rockies that are clear-cut - a logging method that should be outlawed; abandoned mines, with collapsing buildings, broken equipment. rusting cars and garbage everywhere; entire ghost towns - the result of a "boom and bust" economy.

Why don't we have a bond system that requires companies to clean up after themselves and return the area to its natural state when they have to close a mine? Gravel roads, built for clear-cut logging, remain after the loggers are gone - a tremendous waste of land.

Visit any place after 25 years and you will see vast changes. This is called development and it causes the loss of green areas to the growing population. Canada does not have much green space left; all is huge cities, factories, farms and ranches. Only in the mountains, and the far north, does some green still exist. In the opinion of many, the Rockies should be protected - either by enlarging existing National Parks, or by creating new ones. Most of our beautiful lakes are surrounded by development and summer homes - placing the lake in the center of town. The water is polluted; the wildlife has long since fled - all for the sake of a few people who want to visit their cottage a few times a year. How does that make sense?

We all must have three cars, boats, motor homes, ski-doos and, of course, electric nose hair trimmers. We are afflicted by a modern disease called Affluenza - a very contagious, and apparently incurable disease that makes us want more and more. The Joneses have it, so we must have it too - whatever it is. Why does North America consume over 50% of the world's energy and consumer goods? Consume? Why not call it what it is - waste! Why must 6% of the world's population use over 50% of its resources? It is not just Affluenza - it is insanity!

People must realize that, by wasting so much, we create massive pollution and, in effect, dig our own graves. Picture winter - cars idling for an hour, windows and single-layer glass doors half-open. Does this happen because of cheap energy or a lack of thought?

People trample grass in city parks, along sidewalks and elsewhere. A fortune is spent to re-seed the grass and re-sod the parks. Wouldn't it be wiser to walk on the sidewalks and use the money we save for hospitals and schools?

The same people, who do these things in the city, drive into the wilderness and behave in exactly the same way. The result is destruction and the sad thing is, they don't know any better: they trample the meadows, pick the flowers and leave garbage behind.

Some sufferers of Affluenza seem to think that the more stuff they accumulate, the better the person they become. It is just the opposite: what matters is the kind of person you are - what are your principles and convictions; are you kind and noble? That is much more important than how much stuff you have.

A hundred years ago, this planet was 75% green. People were happy, healthy and lived wholesome lives. Today, less than 30% of the land is green. Some countries have managed to destroy nearly all their green lands. Today we have AIDS, flesh-eating bacteria, and too many retarded people. One woman in eight gets breast cancer and far too many people are half dorks. Why is this happening?

Man cannot exist without nature, and our "more - more" "fast - fast", all-tolerating lifestyle is killing us. Is there any hope? Any cure?

Yes. Slow down. Forget the Joneses. Take a holiday - go for a long hike in the woods. When you find nature, you will find yourself - we are all a part of nature. By killing nature, we kill ourselves. What we need now, is to reduce the world's population, reduce mindless consumerism and get back to where we have 50 - 60% green space on this planet.

We must pressure the government to enlarge our current national parks and create new ones. We must donate money and time to nature conservancy organizations - they will buy green lands and preserve them from development. Leave a green legacy.

Teach your children the words of H.D. Thoreau, who said, over a hundred years ago, "In wildness is the preservation of the world." Teach them respect for nature and encourage them to plant a few trees every year.

Only a green world is a healthy world.

Front cover: Yellowhead Mtn. and Witney Lake, Mount Robson Park
Back cover: Lake O'Hara, Yoho National Park

Design: George Brybycin
Typeset: K & H United Co.
This book was created in Canada
Printed in China by Everbest Printing Co.

For current list, please write to:
GB PUBLISHING, Box 6292, Station D,
Calgary, Alberta Canada T2P 2C9

Photographic studies by George Brybycin :
The High Rockies, Colourful Calgary, Our Fragile Wilderness, The Rocky Mountains, Banff National Park, Jasper National Park, Colourful Calgary II, Wildlife in the Rockies, Rocky Mountain Symphony, Enchanted Wilderness, Wilderness Odyssey, Rocky Mountain Symphony II, Romance of the Rockies, Calgary - The Sunshine City, The Living Rockies, Cosmopolitan Calgary, Banff and Jasper N.P., The Rockies: Wildlife, The Majestic Rockies, Emerald Waters of the Rockies, The Canadian Rockies Panoramas, Eternal Rockies, Calgary, the Stampede City and Environs, Alpine Meadows, The Rockies - British Columbia - The North, Rocky Mountain Odyssey, Banff & Jasper National Parks II, The Canadian Rocky, The Canadian Rockies Panoromas II.

George Brybycin's collection of 20,000 35mm colour slides is FOR SALE.
Subjects include: The Rockies, Western and Northern Canada, Calgary, The 1988 Olympics, Alaska, The Western U.S. and the World. Also available is the collection of all 29 George's books. Offers may be tendered to GB Publishing at the address above.